Short Stories & Tidbits
by Burton Rice, Esq.

Printed and bound in the United States of America
First printing • ISBN 978-0-9991508-7-0
Copyright © 2017

All rights reserved. No part of this book may be reproduced, stored in a retrieval system, or transmitted in any form or by any means without permission from the author, except by a reviewer, who may quote briefly in a review.

Short Stories & Tidbits

by Burton Rice, Esq.

FOR ORDER INFORMATION VISIT
www.scottpublishingcompany.com

SCOTT COMPANY PUBLISHING
P.O. Box 9707 • Kalispell, MT 59904
Toll Free: 1-800-628-0212
Fax: 1-406-756-0098

Dedicated to Diane, my loving wife for 46 years. A better companion and friend could never be found by any man.

About the cover art
The Wandering Buffalo

In 1951, I was 19 years old. The Korean War had started and I knew I would soon be drafted. Shakespeare had written "to be or not to be", but the draft board said "one-A", which meant the Army wanted me. At that time I was the type of person who didn't like to be shot at, so I had decided to enlist. The Air Force would take me, although I never did find out why. I was sent here, there and everywhere, and after almost four years, they thought they had about as much as they could take. I really don't know why, but they gave me an honorable discharge. What a surprise!

The same year I enlisted, my dad bought two buffalo heifer calves. He was going to crossbreed them with our Hereford bull. It didn't work because the bull was afraid of them. After some time, the buffalo would take off whenever they felt like it. They could jump over our fence with ease. It was well known we had them, so the neighbors would call and let us know where they were at. One time they wore out four horses chasing them back. The family enjoyed hearing the stories anyone told them about their encounters with the buffalo. That is, everyone except my mother.

My dad died in July 1955. The buffalo stayed close to home until December 1955. On a Sunday morning they took off and stopped in a farmer's yard seven miles away. The farmer came to our place to tell us about it. When I opened the door, the first thing he said was, "Say, you aren't missing a couple of buffalo are you?" I had fed the cows that morning but hadn't noticed the buffalo, which wasn't uncommon because they always stayed back out of sight until I left. I told the guy I'd be right up there to chase them home. It wasn't too cold, about 20 above, with a wind out of the northwest between five or ten miles per hour. I should have loaded my horse on the truck and hauled him to his place. It took almost an hour to get there on horseback, so I was starting to become a little chilly. I could have warmed up in the farmer's house but I didn't think of it. I had no trouble getting the buffalo starting for home because I think they wanted to go. My horse "Dan" easily kept up with them, except when we came to a fence and they simply jumped over it, but I either took the fence down or looked for a gate. When we got home, they ate some hay and looked like "happy campers", though maybe not as happy as I was. My mother said, "That's it, we're gonna have them butchered." The local butcher shop owner had two sons who came out and did the job in our barn. They bought one and we got the other. We ate buffalo meat all that winter of 1955 and 1956.

This story is 100% true.

Backward

I didn't have the nerve to call this a Forward to my book. This book was written for people under nine years of age. Most people over nine are too sophisticated for anything I might write. Some of these stories are mostly true, others are mostly fiction. I have embellished some of the true ones. That is one of our rights. It is called "Freedom FOR the Press." Being retired, I have a lot of time on my hands. I sleep eight hours a day and idle away the other eighteen. Wait! That's twenty-six hours. I never was good at math.

WARNING: Do not read any part of this book before driving, as it may cause drowsiness!!

I have worn many hats in my lifetime. I'm not sure which one fits the best. I didn't get past "just so-so" in any of them. I farmed and ranched to start with, was in the bowling alley business, peeled logs until my rotator cuff went bad, went to school at DeVry U, worked at Semi-Tool for two years, was secretary-treasurer for a men's golf league for eight years and married for 46 years, but the best thing I can say about my life is that all my kids love me.

A Nickel in the Dirt

The stock market crashed in 1929. I was born in 1932. My dad was renting a small farm in northeastern Montana. We were sharecroppers. Because of poor farming practices and lack of rain, the crops were very poor. The price you got for your grain wasn't worth the gas it took to haul it to town. Most farmers fed it to their livestock. Some didn't plant the seed, fearing it wouldn't germinate. The fields were very dry and about twice a week we would have a dust storm. The 1930s went down in history as "The Dirty Thirties". There was no greenery of any kind in our yard. It was just bare ground. The only reason we made a decent living was because my dad got a job on the WPA. It was a federal government works program to help farmers survive. In our case it was to help maintain roads.

One day I found an old pop bottle and pushed it in the yard, making as I imagined, roads and trails. It was then I saw the nickel! I couldn't believe my eyes. How could I be so lucky? I was overjoyed. I was so elated I ran into the house to tell my parents. Wow. Now I could buy an ice cream cone. At that time, the movie theater in Plentywood showed free movies to kids at a Saturday matinee. The movies were free, but a bag of popcorn cost a nickel. I had a decision to make – a bag of popcorn or ice cream. I didn't have enough money for both. My, how times have changed. But isn't it strange, how something so simple as finding a nickel in the dirt could bring so much joy to a little boy.

This story is about 90% true.

The Busted Cinch

A cinch is a strap connected to the saddle, then tied to the saddle on the other side. It could be made of leather or some other material. On my saddle it was heavy cotton cords. They are attached to a metal ring at each end. The one ring is a permanent fixture on the saddle. The other hangs loose, until it goes under the horse's belly and is strapped to the other side. Some horses get wise to this and extend their belly. When you finished, they would relax their belly and the saddle would be loose. You would try to catch them unawares and tighten it again. Now if you had been riding for awhile and decided to take a break, have a cup of coffee or a beer, you would loosen the cinch. This would not be the case for a bank robber. If he came running out of the bank and put his foot in the stirrup to get on the horse, the saddle would slide sideways and he would end up in the dirt. Not good for a bank robber!

In the busted cinch incident, my saddle was ten years old and the cinch had never been changed. From the horse's sweat and normal wear and tear, it was deteriorating. In fact, one cotton strand had already busted. For normal use it would have been fine. I went out to check the cows one day. I wasn't expecting anything unusual. I was riding "Sonny Boy", a palomino who was a very good cuttin' horse. I was riding along our fence line about two miles from home, and spotted one of our cows in the neighbor's pasture. There were about ten or so cows of our neighbor's with her. About 150 yards away was a gate. I opened it and started to cut our cow out from the others. This was easy for Sonny Boy. It was, as they say, "right up his alley." The cow took off at a run, right for the fence, with me and the horse after her. When she was about 150 feet from the fence, she made a 90 degree turn towards the gate. Sonny Boy made the same turn, but me and the saddle did not! The cinch had busted, so the saddle and I went flying through the air, landing about 20 feet from the fence. I carried the saddle to the gate and closed it. Because the cow had made it back to our pasture, I debated about leaving the saddle there, but decided to carry it home. Mistake number 17. When I got home, the horse was there, waiting to get into the corral. My brother told me I was nuts to carry the saddle home. We could have driven up with the pickup to get it. He was really right on that one. I was a little sore for a few days, but that was it.

This story is 100% true.

The Hardest I Ever Got Hit

We didn't have a football team when I was in high school, so I never got hit very hard until much later. We did have basketball, but I don't remember getting hit very hard there. After my time in the Air Force, our town had a team in a softball league. There were seven teams, so we got a bye on week eight. The town of Outlook was not in our league, or any league. They had a bunch of good players and played any time they could get a game. We got a game with them on our off week. Their best player was Roald Selvig, you could not get a fastball by him. You had to get him out with slow stuff.

For some reason, our catcher didn't show up for this game and we had no reserve catcher. I always played second base, but our coach asked me to catch. It was the only game I ever caught, and I didn't make it through that one. We got Roald out the first time up with slow stuff. I had called for one fastball, way out of zone, which he took. The next time up, we got two strikes on him and I called for a fast one, about a foot outside. Now the pitcher, who just happened to be a human being, made a mistake as humans often do, and the ball came in waist high, middle in and Roald tore the cover off the ball, figuratively that is. It screamed into left center, where the center fielder corralled it and hurled it back in, holding Roald to a double.

We didn't know anything about the next batter, we only knew about Roald. Needless to say, we didn't like what we knew about him. Our job was to get the next batter out. He had hit an outside pitch to right for a single his first time, so I thought we could try to get him out pitching inside. It didn't work! He also hit a liner to left center. There were two outs so Roald took off at the crack of the bat. The left fielder got to the ball and fired a strike to the third baseman. By this time, Selvig had rounded third base and headed for the plate. For just a moment I imagined I saw a locomotive, with smoke billowing out of its stack. The third baseman threw a strike to me, just missing the runner by an inch or two. Of course, I had the plate blocked and Roald came in standing up. That is when the lights went out in Outlook. I saw more stars than there are stars in the sky. I came to about ten seconds later. I was standing halfway down the first baseline. I still had my mitt in my hand, and the ball was still in my mitt. Selvig was out! He came over to me and said he was sorry for not sliding. He repeated it a second or two later. On our team, the on deck hitter was supposed to signal whether to slide or not. I wanted to keep on playing, but the coach told me there was no way I was going to play any more that day. What I didn't know, was I had a bad gash just over my left eye. That is the hardest I ever got hit.

This story is about 90% true.

The Rattlesnake

Most people in Sheridan County believed there were no rattlesnakes north of the Missouri River. They believed that because no one had ever seen one. Good reason! My dad always believed that until I proved it wrong. On an autumn day, my younger brother and I were hunting game birds. We were riding horseback and both of us were carrying 12 gauge shotguns. We were about half a mile from what was called the "Comertown Road." I heard a rattle, looked down and saw my horse had almost stepped on a snake. I told my brother, "That's a rattlesnake." I decided to shoot it. I thought the noise from a 12 gauge would spook the horse, so I had my brother hold him. The blast almost split the snake in two. We went on our way and in an hour or so we had no luck, so we were going to head back home. I was planning on taking the snake with us, but when we got back to him, it looked as if he had moved.

We had a few hired men through the years and they always were telling us half truths and sometimes just plain lies. One of these is that a snake never dies until the sun goes. It didn't matter what you did to it, they never die until sundown. I can't remember if we believed it or not, but I wasn't to touch that snake. When we got home, I told my dad I had shot a rattlesnake. "No you didn't," he said. "There are no rattlesnakes north of the Missouri River."

"Well, I shot one," I said and between the two of us, we finally convinced him that I shot something. We drove up to where the snake was, but he didn't believe it was a rattler. I guess if you believe something for so many years, you have trouble thinking different, even if it's right in front of your eyes. Either somebody called my uncle or he just happened to show up, but his wife had lived in Billings for some time and seen many rattlesnakes. I think maybe she convinced my dad it was a rattler. The local newspaper found out about it and it appeared in their weekly edition, because it was rare. The Westby School heard of it and wanted to put it in the library there. They put it in a two quart jar with a solution to preserve it and it was still there when Becky, my daughter, graduated from high school many years later. But what the "experts" figured was that some farmer up by Comertown was hauling hay from south of the Missouri, the snake was in the hay, had fallen off the truck and made its way to where I shot it.

This story is 100% true.

The Poor Porcupine

We didn't have many porcupines around our farm. More often than not, we saw the results of a fight with a dog. We pulled many a quill from our dogs' nose. It was almost always where they got it because they would come up behind them sniffing away. Whap! That tail would come around, and the dog would run home yelping all the way. I guess we should have taken them to the vet, where they could have got a shot to prevent infection, but we never lost one. Most times, it only happened once to the same dog.

One day, during haying season, I was cutting oats with a swather. I had it set to cut about six inches off the ground. The oats were really thick, it was a 16-foot cut and I couldn't see the ground. I had made fours around the field, came on fifth round and saw a porcupine. He was a strange looking sight. The round before I had clipped all the quills off his back, but he still had them on his sides and tail. If I had been cutting lower, it would have been bad news for that poor porcupine. He seemed fine and was running along the side of the oats that hadn't been cut.

This story is 100% true.

A Snowstorm in May

Some snowstorms are known for their severity, some for their length and some for the time of year. The one that sticks out in my mind happened in the month May. This was in the late 1950s. It wasn't real cold and there was just a slight wind. My brother and I had about a hundred head of cows. We were done calving when the storm hit. There had been two weeks of nice weather and there was very little snow on the ground. Forecasting weather wasn't as good as it is now, so we had no warning and it took us by surprise. The cows were in our spring pasture, almost two miles from home. The cows didn't come home, so we took a load of hay to them. We didn't want to feed there so we just turned around, headed home and the cows followed. There were about ten calves that couldn't keep up, so we unloaded the hay back home, then went to get those ten. This took about an hour. We loaded the calves in the wagon and headed back. The ten cows with missing calves were looking for them. We passed them on our trail, but they kept going. It was getting confusing. So we got the calves back home, unloaded them and then I saddled my horse and got the ten cows back. All I can say is "all's well that ends well."

This story is 100% true.

The Alphabet

When you went to school, did you struggle in English class? Did you hate grammar with a passion? Were you a teenager before you could recite the alphabet? If any of these are true, you might enjoy this little bit.

Any time Anna asked Alice anything at Atlanta's airport, Alice acted as an aroused animal, aiming arrows at anybody.

Burt's black beagle bent backwards by Bob Barker, barked before Betty Baker beat Barbara Benton by Brooklyn Bridge.

Careful Cindy cautioned careless Chris constantly chewing caramel candy, conducting choirs carefully.

Diane, Dominique and Dawn detailed a Dodge in Detroit, depositing dirt and dust in Dover, Delaware during daylight December days.

Elaine enjoyed everyone, eagerly eating eggs

except European egotists.

Friendly Frank found Francis Fonda, firmly fixed frozen feet fourteen fathoms from frosty Finland.

Gentle giant, Gene Greeberg, gave gifts galore, graciously going great guns.

Howard Hawkins hastily handed Henry Higgins his hardhat in Hawaii.

Inept Ivy initially invited Imogene inside Ingrid's igloo in icy Iceland.

Jeremy just joined Jerry's Japanese joyful journey, jogging and juggling James' jars in Jamaica.

Kayla's kennel kept kangaroos kicking kosher kings in Kenya and Kathy knelt knitting kinky kimonos, keeping knobby knuckle kaput.

Lee laughed loudly, likely looking at lovely Lolita's legs in Lafayette, Louisiana.

Mary Martin missed Monday morning's meeting, making more mistakes mimicking magpies in Missoula, Montana.

Nancy Newman never noticed Naomi Nixon numbering neighbors in Nevada.

Oliver O'Conner owned one ornery ox on occasion offering odds opposite of official orders in Oregon.

Peter picked peanuts, packed peaches, printed papers, padded pillows, planted peas, promptly pickled purple peppers, pursued pickpockets, purchased pancakes, praised perfect people, parked pickups, pleased parents, planned perfect parties, pampered pious preachers, placed pretty penguins perhaps pleasantly, all in Pittsburg, Pennsylvania.

Quiet quail quickly quit quivering quote Quaid in Quebec.

Rebecca roasted a red rooster regularly raising radishes religiously in Russia.

Sarah smiled sweetly singing softly selling southern Spain safely sometime Sunday.

Tuesday Takara tried to teach twenty-two temporary tutors to tell time twice.

Uma Underwood used umbrellas unloading unique uniforms in Utah.

Victor Vereen visited various vagabonds vigorously in Vietnam vanishing vertically.

Wanda will work Wednesday, without wondering where Wilma went wrong wanting wisdom.

Xena x-rayed xerox machines in Xanadu.

Young yellow yaks yearn yearly yowling "yahoo!"

Zany Zelda zigzagged zealously in Zaire.

A "B" Story

Burt's brother told him about the birds and the bees. But he went to a bar and bought some beer, then to the butcher's to buy a brisket of beef and a little bacon. At the bakery he asked for bread and buns. He paid for a little butter and brought it to the borough of Brooklyn. He went into the barracks and saw his buddy, Buster Black. Buster told him about his brother Ben who had just passed the bar exam. Ben was going to be a barrister in Brighton, Britain. Burt then went to see the Braves play baseball in Buzzard's Bay, but he was too busy. He went to Boston to be a bat boy, but his belly was too big. Beau Bromell's boy Buster was busy bullying brothers Bill and Bruce, Beau took a bus to Brocton to box big Brain Baer. The bus ride was bumpy, they bounced all the way. A big boulder was in the middle of the road. He bowed his back to the burden and brought it to the bottom of the barrow pit. He bowed out of the boxing match. The breezes blowing through the boughs in Birmingham gave him a bloody nose so he walked backwards to Bozeman to stop the bleeding. His knees buckled when he watched the boys play basketball in Butte.

He bought a big bouquet of buttercups for Betty Blankenship, but there was a butterfly in it so he told her to bring it back before breakfast. He let a balloon fly in Bristol, but a brown bird flew into it and it busted. By and by he bit into a biscuit at the banks of a bayou in Bangkok. He married his beautiful bride, Bridget Bronson in Belgium. They had a bouncing baby boy in Bangor. They named him Chad (oops). He was going to fly a biplane in Beirut, but it busted off before he got there. "Bless you," he said when Barbara Benton blew out her birthday candles. He flew a B-29 in the big one. He played bass in a band in Billings before going to Broadway. He built a barricade of bricks to stop the blackbirds. He was accused of bigotry in Bigfork, made to walk a balance beam. He held onto a banister so he wouldn't have to beg. Big deal! His boss wanted him to buy a Buick. He bounced a check at Benson's bank in Boise. He jumped into the Bay of Biscayne, but the bailiff found him. His bail was a billion so he beat on the bars. He thought he saw "C" on the horizon and carelessly fell on a cot in the Congo. That's when he woke up.

I gave this story a "B"

The Coldest I Ever Was
(in the late 1950s and early 1960s)

My brother and I were helping our mother on her farm. We had the usual machinery, but our truck was getting old. I bought a truck on my own and used it to take the load off the other. I made some money once in awhile using it to haul something for the neighbors. It was late in the year, maybe November, when a friend called and asked if I could haul ten cows he had bought at the stockyards in Sydney. I had hauled a load of coal for my brother the day before and hadn't unloaded it yet. I was going to say no I couldn't, but my brother told me I could use the old farm truck. Sydney is 100 miles from our place and another 12 to my friend's. The old truck was a cab-over Chev, and it ran good all the way to the stockyards. We loaded the cows and headed back.

We had gone about 25 miles when a piston rod broke! I managed to get to the side of the road. We hitched about ten miles to Culbertson, where I called my brother and told him to find somebody to tow us home. We must have sat in a café there for two hours until a friend of ours showed up with a truck to tow us. So we went the ten miles back, hooked a 25-foot log chain to both rigs and took off. Now, I couldn't use my heater, and there was no sense in two of us getting cold, so they both rode together. In 30 miles or so, I was getting chilly. We still had 30 miles just to get to Plentywood. About five miles south from "The Blue Moon" nightclub, which was two miles from Plentywood, I was starting to shiver. My brain must have been frozen because I never thought to honk the horn that something was wrong.

I'm sure that I was the happiest man on the face of the earth when they drove past the turnoff to my friend's place and pulled into The Blue Moon. We stayed about an hour so I could warm up. I don't remember if I borrowed another light jacket or not, but we were on a side wind and not right against it. I didn't get cold, even though we still had about 30 miles to go. We got the cows unloaded and because it was so late, we stayed overnight right there.

This story is 100% true.

Twenty Questions

In the late 1940s and early 1950s, there was a half hour radio program called Twenty Questions. It came on at 6:00 PM on Saturday night. My dad liked the show and didn't mind if we quit early. There was a host and three panelists. The host would name a subject and the panel would try to guess what it was in twenty questions. They were told what it was made of, either vegetable, animal or mineral, or any combination thereof. These subjects could range from the Statue of Liberty to some fictional character. By fifteen questions, they usually had it almost nailed down. The last five were to name it specifically. Once in awhile they missed. They usually had time for three subjects. For the first two, the radio audience was told what it was. On the third they had to figure it out. The program went nationwide and was very popular. I never found anyone who was interested in Twenty Questions for the first three years I was in the Air Force. I was sent to Smokey Hill Air Force Base in Salina, Kansas my last year of service. There was another instrument mechanic who loved it as much as I did. He would introduce the information, and I would be in the cockpit taking the readings for accuracy. This would take thirty minutes. We were connected by two-way radio. We would spend over two hours playing Twenty Questions.

This fellow was married and lived off the base. Every now and then he invited me for supper, and we always played Twenty Questions. One time I got the answer with one question! This is how it happened. One night, after we had eaten, he asked his wife to play. It seems she was intimidated by how fast we went, so he asked her to pick a subject and we would ask the questions. They had a pet cat and it walked by just before she picked her subject. When we asked her if it was animal, vegetable or mineral, she told us it was animal. I blurted out, "Is it that cat?" Of course that's what it was. My friend sighed in disgust. I'm not sure why, but

I think I could have made a good guess. After I got out of the service, I never found anyone who liked that game as well as I did.

This story is 100% true.

We now delve into the magical world of fantasy. In other words, the stories that are almost all fiction.

The Dead Camel

For a short time, we lived in Roanoke, Texas. There was my wife and I, our son Lee and two of our daughters. The other daughter lived in Kalispell. Lee worked for a company that put up tents, and our two daughters were in high school. When Lee was little, he would bring home small animals of all kinds. As he got bigger, these animals also got bigger. Our two girls always dressed nice and presented a pleasing appearance. The same could not be said for their room. There must have been a floor there but I never saw it. It was littered with blankets, pillows, school papers, party clothes, and you name it.

On this particular day, the girls had gone to a birthday party and Lee was working somewhere, so my wife and I were going out to eat. We still had over an hour, but I was an early bird. I couldn't find the hair brush, so I went to the living room where my wife was, curled up on the sofa reading a book. I asked her if she knew where the hairbrush was. She said, "Check the girls' room." I knew what I was in for, but it was always a shock. The floor was its usual mess, but there was a larger lump in the middle. It looked like there was a hoof or some such thing in this pile, so I started clearing things from around the object. I got everything away, and to my great surprise I saw it was a camel! Not just a camel, but a dead one! Well, it took my breath away and I couldn't move for a minute or more. Somewhat dazed, I walked back and muttered to my wife, "There's a dead camel in the girls' room." I don't think she understood what I said because she answered, "Well, I wouldn't be surprised." Not knowing what else I could say, I just repeated it. "Well, deal with it," is how she responded. The shock was starting to wear off, so I decided to "deal with it."

I knew I couldn't get the camel out by myself, so I went out to look for help. Two teenagers were playing basketball, one on one, so I asked them if they would like to make $5.00 each for half an hour's work. They said they would, so we went to work. They each grabbed a front leg and I helped with the back end. We stopped to rest right in front of my wife. She kept her book covering her face so she couldn't see what we were doing. I think she knew. After a minute we got the camel outside and hoisted into our dumpster. It didn't go all the way in, with the back legs and the tail hanging out, almost touching the ground. I paid the two boys and they went back to their game. Later on, the wife and I went to eat. I don't know if it was on purpose or not, but she didn't look at the dumpster. When we came back, she did look that way and said, "I see the neighbors are using our dumpster again." I said, "No, that's the dead camel." She turned her head back and we never spoke of it again.

The next time I saw Lee, I asked him how the camel got to our place. He told me he was helping a fellow putting up a big tent. This guy had a small circus with a few animals and some acts. There was a sick camel lying there and the man said he was going to shoot it. Lee didn't think much of that idea. He wanted to see if he could cure it, so he got someone to haul it to our place. He gave it some grain, a little hay and some water, and then somehow forgot it. He had no idea how it got in the girls' room. I couldn't get anything out of the girls, so to me, it will always be a mystery.

This story is about 95% fiction.

Cataract Surgery

When I reached the age of 40, I began to have vision problems. It wasn't real bad, and I was too vain to do anything about it. Every year it got a little worse, and so when I was 45, I bought a pair of reading glasses at the Dollar Store. Once a year I would have to get a stronger pair. At 50 years of age, I finally went to an eye doctor and got prescription glasses. They would last five years and then I would need a new prescription. So it went until I got to 70 years of age. It was then the doctor said I had cataracts, and suggested laser surgery. He said they would just get worse and worse. "You'll barely feel it, and the whole procedure will be over in less than an hour." My brother had the same surgery two years before, so I called him. He said he hardly felt a thing and the best part was, he now had 20-20 vision, so I agreed to the surgery. An appointment was made, and I started to prepare myself. They could only do one eye at a time, and after the first one, you had to wait two weeks before they did the second. The first one went off like clockwork. The nurses do some fiddling around, which takes 15 to 20 minutes, then the doctor comes in, somehow gets a tiny hole in your eye, then takes a small vacuum cleaner and sucks the bad stuff out. I barely felt anything, and of course I had 20-20 vision in that eye.

Two weeks later, I came in for the second surgery. This one did not go very well at all. I was prepped and ready to go. The nurse had one last thing to do, and she was fiddling with my eyeball when it popped out of its socket, fell down and started rolling across the floor. The two nurses got down on their hands and knees trying to catch it. A cat came through the open door, spotted the eyeball and swallowed it whole. The cat was rushed to a vet, who cut it open. The eyeball was intact with not a scratch on it. They brought it back, cleaned it up and put it back in its socket. I didn't think they would go through with the surgery. The doctor said everything looked good, so they finished the job. I now had 20-20 vision in both eyes. But you know, it is quite disconcerting to be sitting in a doctor's chair watching your eyeball rolling across the floor, looking back at you as if to say, "See you later."

This story is 85% fiction.

Methane Gas

Methane gas is formed by the decomposition of vegetable matter. Cows emit a lot of this because when they eat, they don't digest their food. There are other ways methane gas is formed, but this is the one we are concerned with. If the cow eats mostly hay, methane gas is not a problem. If it eats ground grain, it can be. You can let a pig eat grain from a self-feeder, but a cow, no! She will eat and eat till she can eat no more. Soon the methane gas will form and her belly will triple in size. The pressure has to be relieved. If you know how to do this, it isn't too hard. You have to find exactly the right spot, cut a hole in her hide, then insert a tube there and the gas will exit through that tube. Our neighbor had a self-feeder for his hogs. He had it where they could get at it, but the opening to get into it was too small for a cow. Somehow a cow got in, probably by someone who was careless. Before anyone saw her, she got her fill and a lot more. No one knew what to do, so they called my dad. He didn't have any ideas, but my older brother had worked at a feedlot and seen the operation that relieves the pressure. He warned us that methane is highly explosive. The news of this cow had gotten around and several people came to look at her. One of them was a young feller, about 25 years old. He hadn't shaved for a couple of days, so he had a slight beard. My brother went to work, the hole was made in the cow's hide, and the tube was being inserted. At this same time, the young man decided to have a cigarette. He was lighting a match when the gas erupted out of the cow's belly. When it hit the flame from the match, it exploded. It burned off the fellow's beard, his eyelashes, eyebrows and every hair on his head. He got his eyes closed in time, but the place smelled like it would at branding time. The cow was fine, but she never had another calf. One good thing came out of this. The young feller never smoked another cigarette for the rest of his life!

This story is 100% fiction.

Waffles

I had known Jerome and Caroline for over twenty years. I always admired them because they scrimped and saved for more than fifteen years so they could send their youngest child to college. Jerome told me about their trip when they took her to the college. They hadn't bought a car in over a dozen years. This one was acting up a bit. On the way back, Jerome saw a sign for a town about a mile off the road. It said they had all the services. He drove in front of the garage and saw a mechanic. He said, "It sounds like a bad fuel pump." They didn't have any, so would have to send for one, and Jerome and Caroline had to stay overnight. There was a nice looking hotel about two blocks away. They checked into their room, cleaned up a bit, and went to the hotel's restaurant to eat. The waitress came over and told them the evening's special was waffles. Jerome told her he wanted a sirloin steak, medium rare. His wife ordered prawns. The waitress said, "And with that, you can have waffles." Waffles didn't sound good with their meal, so they declined. After they finished eating, the waitress told them there were waffles for dessert. There was a guy at the counter who chipped in, "Try the waffles, they are good." Jerome was a wondering if they had gotten a buy on waffle batter.

They left for their room, hoping they could get going the next day. They slept in the next morning, not getting up until almost 10:00. They weren't very hungry, so they were going to get something light. There was a new waitress that morning, and she told them the special was waffles. The same guy was at the counter again, just nodding his head up and down. Jerome ordered two slices of toast with bacon. Caroline had toast and jam. After eating, they went to see if the parts came in for their car. The mechanic said, "You should have ate the waffles." Jerome thought there must be something about those waffles, that some locoweed had gotten into them and everybody went crazy or got addicted.

He asked about the parts, but they wouldn't be in for about three hours. They strolled around town but there wasn't much to see, not being a tourist attraction. They sat down on a bench in the park, watched the squirrels, listened to the birds sing and the children playing. Every now and then a couple would walk by, and they could hear them mutter, "Those are the people that won't eat the waffles." About 3:00 they decided to get something to eat. There was a new waitress and as soon as they walked in, she said, "Your waffles will be ready in a few minutes."

"Whoa, wait a second," said Jerome. "We don't want any waffles." The guy who was always there hopped off his stool, came over to them and said, "Listen fella, we've taken all we're going to take off you. We've been real nice, but now you are either going to eat waffles or you are going to spend the night in jail." Jerome laughed at him and said, "You can't put anyone in jail for not eating waffles." The guy said, "I can go out and get four or five people, go to City Hall and in a half hour, have a law enacted that says you either eat waffles or you spend the night in jail, so it's your choice my friend." Jerome looked at his wife, she shrugged her shoulders and said, "I guess we can eat waffles." Jerome didn't want to give into something that stupid, but he didn't want to spend the night in jail.

There wasn't anything great about them, they just tasted like, you know, waffles. When they were finished, everybody in the place was smiling, nodding approval, and they even got a round of applause. You would have thought they had just saved the town from a disaster. They went to see if their car was ready. The mechanic was just beaming at them. "I am glad you ate the waffles," he said. Jerome wanted to get out of this lunatic town as fast as he could, so he paid his bill and quickly left. Any time they went to see their daughter after that, they always made sure the car was running good. For almost two years after that, Jerome would have a dream, two times a week, where he would be chased by a couple of waffles down a dusty road. Just before they caught him, he'd wake up.

This story is 100% fiction.

Calving

I was helping my dad on his ranch in the spring of 1955. Most of the calves had been born by the end of April. There were ten cows that were late, and among these was one heifer, just two years old. A lot of heifers have trouble giving birth, so we kept a close watch on her. The late cows were kept in a small pasture close to home. Early one morning, I spotted the heifer trying to give birth, and she wasn't having much luck. I thought I night have to help, so I stuck around. She was laying in a small gully, about five feet deep with long sloping sides. I was riding a horse named "Dan", who wasn't completely broke. He wasn't "ground hitched", which means if you dropped the reins, he'd be gone, headed for the barn. The calf just wasn't coming out, so I knew I would have to pull it. I didn't have a rope with me, so I had to use my belt. I took my belt off, and oops, my pants fell down around my ankles. I had to hold onto the reins with one hand, and try to make a loop with my belt to put around the calf's legs, which were just showing. Somehow I managed to do it. I didn't think of it at the time, but what a picture that would have made. A guy standing with his pants around his ankles, holding bridle reins with one hand and trying to pull a calf with a belt in the other.

I thought it was going to be a struggle, but on my first pull, the calf came right out. A lot of mothers don't like something messing with their babies, so it was best if I got out of there. I couldn't get on the horse because my pants were down by my ankles and one hand was holding the reins, so I hobbled halfway up the gully, stopped to look back, and the cow was licking her calf. I got the rest of the way up the slope. I found an old stump, and wrapped the rein around a broken branch. I pulled my pants up, put the belt on, and did a survey of the situation. The calf was getting a drink of that good fresh milk. The first few days, the milk had colostrum in it, which is real rich in protein and antibodies. When this milk goes through her body, the mother will always know which calf is hers. I checked the rest of the cows and all were fine. When I got back home, I told my dad what happened, leaving out one part. I think you can guess which one that was.

This story is 100% fiction.

A Ridiculous Story

About twenty years ago, I wrote a ridiculous story. Now after twenty years, I have read a multitude of these types, and I have concluded that mine is the most ridiculous of all time. You can be the judge, so here it is.

It's about a disease that only five people have had. At least that's how many have been reported. I am the only one who survived this horrible malady. Everyone will get this sickness when they get to 200 years of age. Very few people, do! About a week before your 200th birthday, you feel yourself getting warmer and warmer. At the exact time of your birthday you burst into flames! Everybody who got it tried to put out the fire, either wrapping themselves in a blanket or something, or if there was water thereabouts, trying to douse it out that way. Wrong, wrong,

wrong. That only makes it worse. Quite by accident, I did the correct thing. I noticed I was getting warmer as I approached 200. I planned to go to the doctor the afternoon of the day I turned 200. I was doing some chores in our barn in the morning, and that's when it happened! All of a sudden I was on fire. I was dumbfounded as to what to do. Of course the barn caught on fire. I just wandered around in a circle. I didn't know it at the time, but that was the only thing that would help. After a moment, the fire went out. To my surprise, I had no burns or scars or marks of any kind. I was a pretty lucky fella. Here is a warning to you! When you get close to 200, be prepared. Get inside a wooden structure, and if it doesn't start on fire itself, if you want to live, be sure to set it on fire yourself. Believe me, I am not looking forward to my 400th birthday.

If you can prove to me that there is a more ridiculous story than this one, I will give you my gold watch. It will be hidden somewhere, but there will be clues to help you find it.

P.S. The name of the disease is: Bi-Lentennial Trichinosis.

This book has three basic parts. The first part, the stories, are mostly true. The second are those that are mostly fiction. The third are just some random thoughts, limericks, and dis, dat, and da udder ting. We'll start with:

Appearances Can Be Deceiving.
(Or You Can't Judge A Person From Behind)

As I am writing this, I am 85 years old. This deceives a lot of people, they think I am only 83. I won't say anything about those who think I am 87. Two years ago, when I was actually 83, I decided to go golfing. I was in very good shape at that time, physically, that is. I got to the golf course, opened the trunk, and was leaning over to take my clubs out. I heard a car drive up behind me. It stopped and a woman's voice said, "What are you doing after you finish golfing?" I turned around and when the woman saw how old I was, her chin fell about six inches. She looked dazed, confused and embarrassed. I said, "Nothing, how about you?" She pushed the accelerator pedal all the way to the floor, burned rubber, and was out of sight before I could blink an eye. Appearances can be deceiving!

Insecurity

Why do some people try to impress other people? They almost always sound or act stupid. I think it's because they are insecure. I wish I had a dollar for every time I acted stupid. I'd be a millionaire.

Limericks

I think limericks began in Ireland. It sounds like something the Irish would do. I loved limericks, so about three months ago I tried my hand at writing a few. I got carried away at it and before I knew it, I had written about 50 of them. I took a break, and reread them. It was then that I discovered I was no good at what I was writing. The limericks were no good! Here are two that were written by a professional:

> The Reverend Henry Ward Beecher
> Called the hen a most elegant creature.
> The hen, pleased with that
> Laid an egg in his hat
> And thus did the hen reward Beecher.

If I was a critic, I would give this a grade A+.

The other limerick goes like this:

> There was a young lady from Niger
> Who smiled as she rode on a tiger.
> They returned from the ride
> With the lady inside
> And the smile on the face of the tiger.

This limerick, I also give an A+.

Now here is the best of those that I wrote:

> A stranger came to our town one day.

It was in the very last part of May.
She was tall and thin
And drinking gin.
Needless to say, she had a great day.

I wanted to give a grade, and my logical mind told me it was barely worthy of an F, for failure. I tried to write F down, but my vision was blurred, my hand was shaking and I couldn't see what I was writing. When my vision cleared, I looked to see what I had written. It was a D-. What happened is, vanity raised its ugly head, and it wouldn't let me give a failing grade to something I had written. Like it says in the Bible, vanity, vanity, all is vanity.

Mistake Number 212
(Or If You Prefer Number CCXII)

Earlier I wrote if you were over nine years of age, you might be too sophisticated to enjoy this book. I meant that figuratively. I didn't mean your age in actual years you lived. I meant if you have the soul and essence of someone under nine. Someone 90 years actual age might enjoy this book. 212 mistakes is not the number of errors I made in my life, that would be astronomical. It is how many I have made in this book.

Communication

When I was in high school, I couldn't communicate with girls my age. I wasn't afraid of them, I just didn't know how to talk to a girl. Our teacher for English class was about 45, thirty years older than I was. There was no trouble for me to talk to someone that age. I asked this lady if she could help me. A friend of mine was walking by at the same time, heard our conversation and said, "The best thing to do is to tell them lies and give 'em candy." The teacher didn't like that and uncharacteristically, she said, "Shut up and sit down." She couldn't think of a way to help me, but she would poll the class to find out what the girls' opinion was. There was one girl who claimed to be an artist, so she drew a picture of me that typified the girls' opinion.

Here is that picture

Who Dat Dere?

This picture was circulated through the whole school, so I knew I wouldn't get a girlfriend locally. I had to get out of town.

This story is 95% fiction.

Love

Sixty-five years ago I fell in love with a beautiful young girl. I was too shy, bashful, reluctant, reserved, reticent and silent to do anything about it. And so, alas, it was not meant to be. I guess that old saying is correct, "Faint heart never won fair maiden."

Moods or Personalities

Is a mood you're in part of your personality? I don't know. I'm old, I don't answer questions like that. What I do know, is that horses, especially saddle horses, do have two distinct personalities. One is going away from the barn, the other is coming back to the barn. You would think you had two completely different horses. One Sunday, I rode my horse "Dan" to my uncle's farm. It was seven miles away, and took one hour to get there, even though I was trying to get him to move faster. I spent about two hours visiting, and headed back home. I was now riding an Arabian stallion. I tried holding him back, but my arm got sore, so I finally just turned him loose. It only took 30 minutes to get home.

People have many moods: their early morning

mood, their road rage mood, their drinking mood, which could be anything from morose, combative or talkative, and about 17 others. Very few people have a mood that looks like this:

I wonder what is wrong with these people. Some are like this:

I don't wonder about these people. I fear them.

Stories Not Included

There are two stories I have not yet included in this book. They are mostly true, but the people involved might have a different view. I would let you read these two, but they could not leave my sight, you would have to sign a notarized affidavit, swear on the Bible, cross your heart and hope to die, that you would never breathe a word about what you read. Oh, I almost forgot, there would also be a fee. $25.00 sounds about right. On second thought, make that $100.00, put in an escrow account. After five years, if there had been no lawsuit, you would get your money back with 5% interest, maybe, perhaps, somewhat likely, could happen, over 10% chance.

Not Enough Time

Roy Clark sang a song that had a line that went like this: "There are so many songs in me that won't be sung." I stole a little bit of that line that goes, "There are so many stories in me that won't be told." I just won't live long enough!

150 %

The first 50% of my stories are boring, the second 50% are pure nonsense, and the last 50% are nothing but balderdash. You may have noticed my math ain't no gote, my speiling is atroshious, and my grammer stinks.

Anticipation

I often wonder whether I will bask in the glory of these stories or be embarrassed by the shame of them, or something in between. It is universally understood and accepted by the most profound philosophers that anticipation is the very nectar of human existence. I might go so far as to proclaim that anticipation is the paramount pinnacle of pleasure, so supreme and palatable an emotion that realization is dwarfed by comparison. Wow! What a statement. I'll bet you thought you'd never read something like that in this book. Not to worry, it won't happen again. Why? Because I stole it.

Carpal Tunnel

I have done a lot of writing lately and I don't want to get carpal tunnel syndrome. I hope that is what you call it. I said I was a writer, not a great writer, not even a good writer, just a writer. So if you don't like it, take your sad story of the complaint to a special room where a 95 year old man with ear plugs will keep nodding his head up and down, singing "Old MacDonald Had A Farm, E, I, E, I, O." I'm sure this will satisfy you. I'm not a good writer, nor a good writer's son, but I'll write stories until the good writers come.

If any of these stories have brought a little amusement into your life, a smile to your face, perhaps a chuckle of two, maybe even a tear to your eye, then I have accomplished my mission, and I will say to you, as Jim Reeves sang in a song:

> Adios amigo
> Adios my friend
> The journey we have travelled
> Has come to
> The End

Appendix, or Appendage whichever you prefer

Recommended Books:

Slaughterhouse Five by Kurt Vonnegut
Angela's Ashes by Frank McCourt
Counting Coup by Larry Colton

Thanks to Kayla Johnson and Takara Juntunen, my granddaughters, for their drawings.

www.ingramcontent.com/pod-product-compliance
Lightning Source LLC
Chambersburg PA
CBHW071333190426
43193CB00041B/1763